The God of the Future

The God of the Future

JEFF HOOD

RESOURCE *Publications* · Eugene, Oregon

THE GOD OF THE FUTURE

Resource Publications
An Imprint of Wipf and Stock Publishers
199 W. 8th Ave., Suite 3
Eugene, OR 97401

www.wipfandstock.com

PAPERBACK ISBN: 978-1-5326-3356-0
HARDCOVER ISBN: 978-1-5326-3358-4
EBOOK ISBN: 978-1-5326-3357-7

Manufactured in the U.S.A.   NOVEMBER 6, 2017

For the Kids

Prescript

Are we here?

Pain. Suffering. Abuse. Injustice. Hate. Violence. There is no question that our world is very sick. We all think about it. However, there are consequences for too much thinking. Individuality is dead. No one is free to think. In our society, you can be anything you want to be except different. The only way that someone can assert their independence is by taking their own life. In the midst of the horrors, why do we keep living? We are all curious as to whether the future will be better. Questions propel our feet. Questions keep us alive. Questions are responsible for the crack in every line. Questions killed God and questions will restore something worth living for.

Rev. Dr. Jeff Hood
May 16, 2017

Script

The future is a question.
God is the question.
Where are we going?
Will God be there?

"Jesus, you have violated the laws of the cosmos! For your sins, you are hereby sentenced to disintegration." The cosmic jury had spoken and their ship began to travel closer and closer to the fiery star. When the heat became unbearable, Jesus was shot into the middle of the star. Watching him through powerful viewing devices, everyone laughed and slapped tentacles awaiting his forgone demise. The problem was that Jesus disappeared. Assuming that they just missed the disintegration, everyone blasted off into different directions. Out of sight out of mind. Whether the authorities noticed or not, everyone knew that something had changed. Space seemed so lonely. Darkness grew darker. The planets no longer shined. Was this the end? Then, the star began to shake and quake. There was a beautiful light coming from the center. When everyone got as close as they could, the star exploded. Light overwhelmed them all.

There had never been a brighter light. This was the light. This was the source of all light. Universes filled with promise. There were no dimensions unexposed. All of creation heard the boom. "Lo, I am with you always .. " They were no longer alone.

Is God an Alien?

The light is still speaking. Do you remember? The boom cannot be silenced. Can you see it? Words are written in the stars. Explosions of magic are as clear today as they were then. Can you still hear them? Touch the present. God is there. Touch the future. God is there. Touch the present. God is here. Touch the future. God is here. In the economy of God, present is future and future is present. God is. A journey into our future is a journey into our present. There is no time. There is only future. There is only God.

Are there disciples of the future?

As Jesus prepared to leave the disciples, he assured them that he would never leave them. Though the incarnation takes many shapes, Jesus leaves no doubt that the incarnation is perpetual. Jesus is everywhere in everything. In a resurrected presence, Jesus declared his perpetuity by pointing to the future. There, I believe we will find him.

Is God hiding?

Have you ever walked outside on a clear night and looked up? There is so much to be found. Looking deeper and deeper into the dark sky, you slowly become one with the universe. Desperate to draw close, you rise up on your tiptoes. Closing your eyes, you realize what you are experiencing is beyond sight. Lingering, you don't want to move. Then, you open your eyes and realize that you are returning from the future. Changed by your travels, you proceed into the future. God lives in the galaxies of our dreams. The future pulls us beyond the stars.

Where is the future?

Does God know the future? God is in us and we are the future. Life is something to be lived not known. The future doesn't exist until we create it. God exists. We exist. God is existing. We are existing. God is the future. We are the future. Dreams drive us to unknown futuristic places. Divinity has always dwelled in the unknown. God finds us in our questions and pushes with us into the future.

God is not afraid. We can't be either. We must believe in ourselves. We must believe in God. We must believe in the future. Time travel is possible and it exists within God . . . within us.

How does God travel?

There are nightmares. The future fails. God fails. I'll never forget the sight of thousands of people stranded on rooftops. Food and drinking water was in short supply. Patients died alone in hospitals. The scenes grew worse and worse. The future was lost. God drowned. For much time, all seemed lost. How can a future even be possible? I can't breathe. Then with a splash, hope pushed through. The future was reborn. The greatest means of resurrection for us all is hope. Maybe hope is God. As the past holds us back, hope is what drives us into the future. Hope is what propels us to God. Hope is the future. God is the future. The future never dies. The future is hope perpetual.

Will there ever be a time when God is not?

Early one morning, I saw the light. When you're a child, lights always seem to be bright. What happened to such awe? I stared deeper and harder. The light grew bigger and brighter. As it got closer, fear overwhelmed me. At the last second, I screamed out. No one could hear me. The light had already pulled me in. I didn't know where I was going. I just knew I was no longer there. I wondered if this had anything to do with God? If so, I wondered why I was so afraid? Isn't light supposed to be a calming force? Questions multiplied exponentially. Then, I heard a voice. I looked everywhere to find it. Deep in the middle of time and space, I heard my name. The sun burned in the distance. Planets disappeared. Everything I ever imagined was in reach. Dreams blossomed eternally. I kept reaching for tomorrow. I forgot about today. I heard my name. Then, the beauty stopped and I was alone. Everything changed. Then, everything exploded. There were billions of Gods all calling my name. What's more, the Gods were multiplying.

God never stopped. It was wild. Looking at all the different kinds of God, I realized that God truly is God everywhere. God is not bound to one expression. God is expressionful and expressionless. God didn't happen. God is happening. God is future. Once more, they all called out my name in one voice. I was looking at one God. Through the expressions of billions, I knew that the love of God knows no boundaries. I had seen the future. The future was now in me. I didn't want to leave. I closed my eyes to try to hold it all in. In that exact moment, I opened my eyes. I was lying in bed. Before long, my mom called me down for breakfast. I knew that'd met God somewhere out of this world.

Are dreams the only way?

There is no other way to consider the future of God without considering the future of us. The future is wildly provocative. The future is an affront to our present sensibilities. We will either change or be left in the past. God is hope. Hope draws us beyond what is to what's next. God is to be interpreted through difference and change that is and is not possible. The paradoxes repeat incessantly. God repeats incessantly. God is the same forever. God is changing. The paradox is revealed in the fact that God is. God is what? God is. In the isness of God rests the future. In the midst of our finitude, God reveals to us that God doesn't know the future . . . God is the future. God is the fullness of hope. Theology is about the exploration of the fullness of hope. God travels with us as we meet enlightenment. God learns too. Knowledge always rests in tomorrow.

Do the paradoxes make God?

The last moments in the life of a loved one. The birth of a child. The shots that rang out. Our minds take us on pleasant and unpleasant journeys all the time. Why do we need time travel when we have time travel in our minds? We dodge dinosaurs. We struggle with things left undone. We fight back demons. We travel throughout time all the time. God does too. For, there is nowhere we can travel where God will not be. God lives in our dreams.

Is God a nightmare?

I've always love dreaming about other planets. What are they like? How far away are they? Are they dangerous? What are they made of? How many moons do they have? The questions never stop. When I was in school, I remember learning about each planet in our solar system. We were told what would happen to the body in each environment. From instantaneously burning to death to choking to death to freezing to death, the options were not very attractive. Though we knew about planets outside of our solar system existed, nobody really knew what they were like. As I grew older, we started to learn that there are inhabitable planets all over the universe. I started to travel to these places. With the speed of the mind, I arrived in no time. These other worlds were amazing. They had all that we would ever need to thrive. What if we could move there? Would God join us? God doesn't leave anyone behind. Religious ideas centered on earth would be left on earth. I bet God would have some new ideas to share with us. God has already been there and knew we were coming. Let's not forget, God is the ultimate space traveler. In a universe that doesn't end, imagine how many planets there must be. There is life, life and more life out there. Surely, we don't think that we're the only ones God created in God's image do we?

Can aliens know us?

Doesn't everybody hate getting dumped? Before I met the love of my life/my wife, I'd fallen in partial love many times before. I can remember a particular heartbreak that came at a difficult hour. Things were just not going well. Then, I got blindsided by a phone call that terminated our relationship. After completing everything for the day, I struggled to get home. Once I did, I went across my living room and dropped down on the couch with a thud. Glad that no one could see me, I started to cry. Within a few seconds, my dog raced over to comfort me. I could tell from the look in her eyes that she knew what was going on. My dog's presence in those hours brought tremendous comfort. As I talked to her about everything that happened, I knew she could understand me. I wish that she could have spoken to me. Maybe one day she will. In the last couple of decades, scientists have worked hard to help animals develop communication skills. From teaching sign language to exploring other forms of interactions, scientists are learning more and more. What happens when we arrive at the day when scientists help animals talk and express themselves? It's not as far off as it seems.

Do animals talk dirty?

Not long after the invitation was given, she started coming down the aisle. Everyone was surprised. When she got down to the front of the church, the pastor didn't know what to do. She raised up on her back legs and declared, "What must I do to be baptized?" Everyone froze. Eventually, the pastor got the courage to ask, "Do you want to follow Jesus?" She responded, "I do." Reaching out his hand, the pastor grabbed her paw and led her up the steps. Looking into her eyes, the pastor managed to ask, "Where did you learn to talk?" "I am the product of recent scientific breakthroughs." As they walked down into the water, fur floated everywhere. After a profession of faith, the pastor baptized the dog. Our ability to communicate with animals is rapidly expanding. With increased ability to engage in communication, we will be faced with a number of difficult questions. Should animals be baptized? Do animals have souls? Can animals pastor churches? Can animals recognize their own sin? The questions are endless . . . and we are not prepared for the answers.

Is God a talking ass?

I don't trust the present to tell me what tomorrow will bring. The unknown is always coming. God exists in the unknown. The unknown God that is beyond any God we could ever imagine is pulling us from the present to the future. Everything will be wilder. Everything will be stranger. Everything will be changed. Works about the future are works about the unknown. Works about the unknown are attempts to touch God. On some level, writings about the future will always be conjecture. Nevertheless, conjecture allows us to reach into the darkness and cling to what we find. The future is conjecture and so is God.

Is conjecture holy?

Everyday, the man opened his eyes and waited. With no ability to speak or move, the man simply waited on his caretaker. Blinking was his only means of communication. Sometimes, it was difficult to blink fast enough to get his point across. From baths to eating to taking a shit, the routine repeated over and over again. The man thought about suicide everyday. The only problem was that he didn't have the ability to go through with it. Euthanasia was legal and seemed like his best option. Even in the midst of his misery, he clung to hope that there might be something left. One day, the man was watching television and heard about a new experimental medical procedure. Quickly, he communicated to his caretaker that he wanted to get in touch with the doctor. After extensive communication, the doctor decided to fly out to see him. Warning the man that there were a variety of risks, the doctor shared with him that a successful head transplant would make him well. Knowing that he was dying regardless, the man didn't hesitate. After traveling to a remote location, the doctor started the preliminary procedures. Six weeks after the preparations began, a match died in a car accident. After confirming that the man was comfortable with receiving a woman's body, the doctor administered anesthesia and started the surgery. Dozens and dozens of fellow doctors filled the room. Specialist after specialist worked on their particular areas. Countless hours of surgery culminated in the fusion of the spine. The man was ready for recovery. Doctors were relentless to make sure that the procedure was successful. Many weeks later, the man awoke from his coma. Surprisingly, he felt great and couldn't tell a difference. The only thing that had changed were his much larger breasts and he now had a vagina. Eventually, he gained an ability to live life without any of his prior afflictions. The first head transplant was a complete success. However, multitudes of questions remained.

Does God need a head transplant?

Think this is too Frankenstein to actually happen? Think again. Sooner or later, head transplants are coming. Doctors around the world are already racing to make it happen. Animal head transplants have already happened. What would such a medical development mean for people of faith? The questions only birth more questions. Where does the soul reside? Is it possible to slice up the soul? Is someone responsible for the evil committed by their new head or body? Does the heart have a special relationship to spirituality? How would a new head facilitate old relationships? If heads are swapped, what image of God survives? What does this mean for family relationships? Many have assumed the head is the center of the person and thinking is what makes the person who they are . . . perhaps we don't have enough information to know the answer to such thoughts yet. We will very soon. More questions are coming. Our faith will either adapt or die.

Does God care about our bodies?

God is in the future. All God is . . . God fully is. God doesn't know the future because God is the future. God is growing. God is becoming. As God grows and becomes, God pulls us to grow and become. To live is the greatest spiritual discipline. The courage to live is our future today. God is incarnate in those who incarnate hope. God is hope. Hope is the future. God is the future. To push into the future is to push into God. In our hope for tomorrow, we will find the God of today.

Is God past?

Over the last few years, many have started to realize that our planet is getting increasingly crowded. With rapid reproduction taking place all over the globe, we can only expect such overcrowding to continue. In some parts of the world, overcrowding has led to poverty and wide array of environmental concerns among other problems. While there are a variety of reasons for this phenomenon, there is one that speaks particularly to the relationship between advancement and overcrowding.

Does God suffocate?

Years ago, I conducted research at a hospice facility. Over time, I got to meet and interact with many of the patients. There was a small minority of really old patients who were in long extended comas and were never expected to wake up again. When I asked about these patients, I was told that advances in modern medicine had created a way for people to live a very long time in very poor condition. Though I was there for a considerable amount of time, I didn't see any of these patients die. In the midst of it all, I started to consider the global consequences for advances in modern medicine. In the midst of these really old people at the hospice living a much longer time, the hospice became unable to meet the needs of those who needed hospice care in the area. This is a microcosm of what is coming for us.

How old is God?

Imagine the consequences of life expectancy increasing to 120. This will lead to billions and billions of more people on the planet. There will be an increased need for medical services and facilities.

Can you imagine the increased demand with regard to housing for older people? In the midst of increased demand, prescription drugs will become more and more demand. Will we be able to keep up? While it sure would be wonderful to have people we love around for a longer period of time, are we prepared for the consequences? Aging and crowding are complex issues that lead to a variety of spiritual questions. How can we fulfill our mission to the least of these? How can we have enough resources? How can we love our countless neighbors? Does the image of God become diluted? Can we hear God when all we can here are other people? What happens when silence dies? What happens when no one dies? God is in our increasing population. God is also in their increasing population. Maybe we can work together to solve our problems. Maybe we won't. Sometimes planets collide. Sometimes they don't. Life is worthy of protection no matter what it looks like or where it is from. There is exponential blessing to be found in innumerable images of God. The more the holier. Through our construction in God's image, God is always where life is. Through the death and resurrection of Jesus, God is always where death is. Overcrowding can lead to many blessings. We just have to think about what spirituality looks like when we get there. Could there be another dimension to offer relief?

Who will take care of God?

There is nothing new. Was there ever? Everywhere I look, I see what I have always seen. In the midst of such monotony, I still find something intoxicating about the future. I don't know if it's the unknown. I don't know if it's the divinity of it all. I don't know if it's the creation of it all. I just know that the idea of future gives me much hope that there might actually be something in the darkness.

Is God seen?

God is in the magic of the next. Sometimes magic is scary. We are told to put aside our fears. We must embrace the mysteries of time or no time at all. What is the value of a coming second? God is there. What is the value of a coming minute? God is there. What is the value of a coming day? God is there. What is the value of a coming year? God is there. What is the value of a coming decade? God is there. What is the value of a coming century? God is there. What is the value of a coming millennium? God is there. What is the value of the future? God is there. The future is God's home. God is not. The future is not. In the uncertainty of not, God is. God lives in the notness. The nonexistance of the future speaks to the nonexistance of God. God is. That is it. The isness of God exists in every manner of time and space. No matter what the future is, God is.

Can you touch the notness of God?

"Look!" Strange ships filled the sky. As they got closer, nobody knew what to do. People were screaming and running in every direction. Every television was full of video and commentary. Fire trucks and police cars zoomed around trying to keep calm. Churches filled up. Politicians were trying to assure everyone that they had everything under control. Everyone knew the truth . . . nobody had anything under control. Every country in the world had their militaries on high alert. When the door to the ship finally opened, a purple being slithered out. With a loud voice, the being shouted, "I am here to share the Gospel of Jesus Christ with you." Immediately, people realized that the aliens were here to evangelize us. In time, it became clear that these beings were simply trying to live out the Great Commission they'd received. Jesus had visited their planet about a hundreds of years ago. As they rolled out their scriptures, everyone quickly realized that their Christianity had little to do with the Christ they thought they knew.

Does God need alien evangelization?

What if time is not linear? Maybe there's not a past, present and future as we have always measured it. Maybe there is something more. Think about the future as anything outside of the now. So, future is anything that is other. There is no past. There is only now and future. Maybe an understanding like this would help us to understand how much we can learn from every ounce of time regardless of its location. Knowledge comes from every place that future is. Where there is future there is knowledge. I don't believe in past. I believe in future. The future is all around us. Every piece of newness is a piece of knowledge. I don't believe in a future without knowledge. I don't believe in knowledge without a future. Open your mind . . . the future is there.

Is God a line?

Not long ago, I recalled and reconstructed a story from my past that is still stunningly relevant. A few years ago, I was studying history at the University of Mississippi. I was in a class on Latin America. As we discussed ancient history, I made the observation that we couldn't prove any of this happened. Immediately, I took a step further and further declared, "I'm not even sure we can prove anything has happened." For historians, such observations are a declaration of war. Historians believe that the past can be proven with proper evidence. I believe that the past can be proven with proper belief. Since it is possible that there is no past, we must construct our own past. After about ten minutes of arguing the benefits of such deconstruction with the entire room, my professor screamed out, "God damn it! This is not a fucking matrix Jeff!!!" After that, my professor cleared the room. Immediately, he turned to me and demanded, "What the fuck was that?" "The deconstruction of history." "Well, don't do it again in my classroom." "Time is a relative concept." "Not in my classroom." There is no fundamentalism stronger than the idea of time. Everyone blindly follows time. Perhaps, we have been fooled. Has time taken our minds?. Maybe we are in a matrix.

Has the match already been decided?

Imagine lying down on a gurney and being fitted with a virtual contraption.

The idea is to put you in another world. As you drift in and out of consciousness, the chaplain of the center encourages you to purge all of your evil in the other world. Then, you are there. After walking down the street a short distance, you recognize an attractive woman from the waiting room. Forgetting about your wife, you follow the woman into an alley and have sex with her. You feel every moment. Your crotch is wet. The conscience is disabled. For the next few hours, you go on a killing spree. From babies to the elderly to everything in between, you kill everything. There is blood everywhere. Before you retreat, you start to drink the blood of one of the children. Finally, the police catch up with you. You pull out your grenade launcher and proceed to blow them up. Slamming through an exit, you jump back into consciousness. The doctors inform you that you have been out of it for over 24 hours. Not long thereafter, you begin to fill a tremendous amount of guilt and regret for the way you acted. Murder and adultery are not a part of your constitution. Or, are they? Is it possible that such evil is just dormant within us? Maybe virtual reality is needed to purge us of our sins. Perhaps, virtual reality is the new confession. Should we be held accountable? Does a virtual God exist?

Is this real?

Ultimately, you decide to momentarily go back into the virtual reality. When you arrive, you immediately go to a church and ask for forgiveness. Within the hour, you are baptized. As the water rushed over your skin, you feel a peace that you have never felt before. Now, you walk back toward the exit. God is in you. When you wake up, you feel like you've left it all behind. Is God in you? Did the baptism count? When one is jumping in and out of virtual realities, what is real begins to blur. Realness becomes incredibly relative. What if reality is manipulated? Are the choices made in the midst of manipulation real choices? Is the manipulation of reality a legitimate means of evangelism? Does spirituality and reality go together? To answer such questions we will have to go to other worlds. Existence is changing.

Does God exist in their worlds?

Since God is the source of all creation, God is constantly creating. When we live into the future we are partnering with God. Engaging the future is a spiritual discipline. We don't know what the future will be . . . so seeking the future is an act of faith. The future is an allusion. God is an allusion. In allusions we find God. Regardless of our fear of nothing, we seek what is.

Is God a hologram?

We only use a very small percentage of our brains. What happens when we begin to figure out how to max our brains out? Before you head to the airport, you reach for an old language dictionary on the shelf. Realizing that you haven't needed it for many years, you race to catch the plane. For the next couple of months, you travel all over the world. In every place, you are able to communicate with no problem. There are no words. There are only thoughts. Humanity's minds have developed to the point where everyone can communicate through their thoughts. Since we don't have to think in particular languages, language has become obsolete. The only problem is that there are no private thoughts. Everyone knows everything about everyone. The world is a quiet place. We realize the loneliness of silent noise that God deals with.

Has God maxed out?

The possibilities of the mind are limitless. Imagine sitting in your living room and staring at the remote control extremely hard. With one slight twitch of the finger, the remote control flies across the room and into your hand. One could doubt that humans are capable of such things, but they would do so at their own peril. Who knows what the human mind is capable of? You stand at the top of your stairs paralyzed with fear. The advancements in brain technology have granted everyone the ability to instantly calculate risk. While such thoughts are helpful in planning some things, for many people such thoughts have left them paralyzed. You know it's a big risk to go down the stairs. You can't move. Brain developments could be miraculously positive. Brain developments could also be miraculously evil. How does a world without private thought have personal spirituality? How can a people who engage everything with their minds follow a Jesus who is far beyond the mind? How does a follower of Jesus live without fear when their mind teaches them to fear everything? Does one get closer or further away from God the more developed their brain is? Is it possible to achieve the mind of God at the height of brain development? As the brain develops are we living into the image of God? The possibilities of the brain are limitless. So is our faith. Perhaps, it's important to remember that God is the one who created brains in the first place.

Is God afraid?

Does God live in our brain? Does God live in our heart? Does God live in our nipples? What about our toes? What about our assholes? The human body has many holes and greasy spots that God could reside in. What if we figure it out? What if a God transplant becomes possible? Are you willing to sign up to be a God donor? There are plenty of people in need.

Will God donate the divine organs?

Face transplants are already happening. How much of a human lives in the face? If you love someone, do you follow the face? Is there a soul in the face? Does identity change when faces change? Since God is in us, can God have a face transplant? Maybe there are many faces of God to touch. Who's to say that God hasn't had numerous face transplants? So, what's in a face?

Does God have a face?

Plants keep us alive. Can they feel what's happening to them? Pollution chokes them. Unrestrained expansion destroys them. Will they survive? Maybe they will evolve and become able to defend themselves. Plants with teeth would be a little harder to destroy. Creation speaks of the creator and we are quickly losing our green cannon. Every time we kill a plant, we are killing a part of God. Our future cannot grow without plants. They too are the voice of God.

Is God a plant?

You know the story. From across the room, eyes meet. Slowly walking over to each other, emotions begin to run high. Once they get close, the conversation is unlike any conversation the two have ever had. After getting closer and closer, the two begin to rub up against each other. Finally, they decide to go upstairs. They can't get to the bedroom fast enough. As they start to make love, one of them shrieks in pleasure. The next morning all of his friends can't believe he just had sex with a monkey. Who's to say that humans can't have intimate relationships with humans? Isn't all of creation made in God's image? Animal intelligence is growing. If consent were possible, why wouldn't intimacy be? Are you ready to bless the relationship of an animal and a person? Wouldn't you think that God has already experienced intimacy with animals?

Has God ever had sex with an animal?

How many people can be in a relationship together? The scriptures seem to indicate that tons of people can be together. Why are we so opposed to polyamorous relationships? I don't think Jesus gives a shit. The future will continue to birth a growing acceptance of nontraditional relationships. Those who stand in the way of such progress will be relegated to the past. Are followers of Jesus ready to encourage the marriage of four people? What about when science creates a path to birth children with more than just two parents? In the very near future, such questions will be asked of everyone. People of faith must be people of love. Besides, isn't God in a polyamorous relationship? Haven't you heard of the Holy Trinity?

Does the size of love increase as people increase?

Can you imagine more than one Donald Trump? Can you imagine four Donald Trumps? Can you imagine hundreds of Donald Trumps? Sounds terrifying to me. However, the day is quickly coming when human cloning will be a reality. Perhaps, the day is already here? What if we're able to bring Jesus back? Is a clone a real person? Are clones made in the image of God? Maybe the laboratory will become the new home of God. Clones are coming. God is one.

Is spirituality cloned?

Medical professionals are getting closer and closer to being able to design your baby however you want. Such designer babies would be intended to eliminate all defects. Would such a scenario bring us closer to God's perfection or is difference and defection a key part of God's identity? Can you imagine when such attempts start to go wrong and mutations occur? If the goal is perfection, what happens to imperfection? Would there be a need to eliminate all persons/babies that are not perfect? Notions of the perfection of Jesus will present real problems in such an environment. Everyone will want their child to be just like Jesus. What people don't understand is that we already are. We were made in the image of Jesus. Is a clone of Jesus the savior of the world? Would we worship the clone? Designer children send us down a path of forgetting that perfection is found in imperfection . . . such is the image of God . . . such is God. To believe otherwise is to slaughter God . . . for difference is God.

Can we design God?

Humanity is changing. Are we moving toward what God created us to be or are we moving away from it? God created us to be create. I can't think of anything more creative than to rush into the darkness of the future just to see what you can create. In the darkness, God is creating. The darkness is God's studio. We become human when we build our own studio and give birth to the future.

Is darkness salvific?

Imagine being counseled by your beloved elderly neighbor. For over three years, you have set under her teachings. When you were having marital problems, she helped save your marriage. She is as close as family. The other day reality set in. When you were sitting in her living room, she twitched a little bit and adjusted her neck. Smiling, she said, "I try to be quiet, but I can't help that I'm a robot." No one had any idea. This day is coming. Can you imagine denominational prohibitions against robots? Can you imagine robots hiding their true identity? Artificial intelligence is going to create a whole host of scenarios. "I want to get married to Maria/a robot." "I just had sex with Charlie/a robot." "Harry/a robot is threatening me." "Rosa/a robot and I are pregnant." "Pat/a robot was just voted in as our pastor." "I just killed Grace/a robot." "Juan/a robot wants to take communion." The possibilities of artificial intelligence technology are limitless. Can a soul be created? God creates souls all the time. In creating artificial intelligence, perhaps we're just emulating God's creation of souls? The image of God is transferable from us in our act of creation. Just like humans, robots have the opportunity to love. Can you program a robot to love all the time? If so, maybe Jesus was a robot?

What is a soul?

When something is created in God's image, there is nothing fake about it. Our image of God transfers to that which we create in

God's image. In the future, God's image will continue to incarnate all of creation in a wild assortment of forms. The crazier it gets, the crazier God will get. God will be transformed by the future. In innovating God's image, we are innovating God.

Is the image of God eternal?

Imagine being able to jump on a plane and fly to the other side of the world in less than an hour. Imagine being able to transport yourself to anywhere instantly. Imagine. In terms of transportation, our imaginations are the only limit. In an increasingly globalized world, we are already connected through instant communication. Imagine even quicker communication. Globalization is fueling technological advancements. Spirituality is tasked with helping people cling to intimacy in the midst of chaos. What will this mean in an age were intimacy is gone? The lines of religion have already started to collapse. How will we adapt? The future of spirituality is about the transformation of adaptation. Theology will have to adapt. God already speaks all languages. God already practices all religions. We will have to join her. God is adapting to the times and changing rapidly. Maybe we just simply need to adapt with God?

Can God collapse?

Change is divine . . . when it's coupled with justice. No one should be oppressed or marginalized by the future. Progress for one should be progress for all. In the midst of rapid change, we must be prophets of a just future. There is no other way to find progress. Our redemption will be based on how we treat the least of these as we fall into the future.

Will the poor always be with us?

Pollution is so thick that no one can see. Our reliance on oil has come back to haunt us. The population has exploded. Mutations have caused births to skyrocket. There is nowhere to go. Everything is overcrowded and dying. There is nothing to eat. All the food is destroyed. Death is becoming increasingly painful. All sorts of diseases rule the lands. Everyone keeps looking for an exit strategy. Suicide consistently looks like the best option. The rich are leaving the planet. Nation after nation keeps detonating nuclear and chemical weapons. People keep asking for answers. Why has God done this to us? I thought we were made in God's image. How can God destroy God's self? We need real help. Can the church set up a painless suicide station? We need liturgies to pray for the quickening of death. Life is gone. What happened to justice? Is prayer even worth it? We need hope. We don't need churches . . . they offer us nothing. We need shelter from the storm . . . but the door is always locked. If spirituality can't speak to the malaise, then spirituality is dead. God has committed suicide with the rest of us.

When is the apocalypse?

The death of God is a futuristic concept. In order to move forward, the God of the past always has to die. Sometimes we even have to murder God. Are you prepared to murder God in order for God to survive in the future? We can't allow the weight of God to hold us back. God must die and meet us in the future. A new and more relevant God is always resurrected by the reviving power of tomorrow. Are we willing to kill God? Our salvation depends on it. Get out your knives.

How long does it take for God to die?

After a motorcycle accident, Melissa lost her arm. In the midst of intense mourning, doctors approached her with the option of getting a bionic arm. Not even considering the consequences, Melissa jumped at the chance. Six months later, Melissa's arm started to do strange things. Before she knew it, the arm took on a life of its own. Ultimately, the arm hit her child. Concerned by what could happen next, Melissa decided to have the arm removed. As such technologies become more and more available, bodies are going to become increasingly unpredictable. Is someone responsible for something they did not do? How do you tell what did what? What if a bionic feature kills someone? People will get bionic eyes in the backs of their heads. People will get eyes anywhere and everywhere. What does an eye on someone's ass see? Some will get bionic sexual organs. What if someone is being discriminated against due to their multiple foot long penis? Is it possible to control eight arms? Is God threatened by such extreme bionic modification? Are we? Are bionic functions even helpful? In the future, bionic manipulation is going to become dangerous. No matter the situation, we must be patient. No modification can destroy the image of God.

Can God be controlled?

Is the future about the past? Is the past about the future? What exists in both spaces? Many claim that God does. Is such a multiplicity of existences possible? We have existed in both. We have a past and we have a future. Maybe we are the existences of God?

Is God behind or ahead?

Humanity's addiction to nuclear weapons destroyed it all. People repeatedly choked to death in the streets. God was no longer present. Death was the only God. Death was the only hope. Is life meaningful when everyone is rushing toward death? We are most human and most divine when we engage catastrophe. Can you imagine how much catastrophe God has seen? Such catastrophe has never destroyed God. Perhaps, it can't destroy us. If you survived an apocalyptic event, would the decline of human existence bring about the end of your faith or would it be just the beginning? Can faith survive? Would you still follow God if you were the only one left? Maybe solitude is God?

Will God be the last one?

The future will bring all sorts of challenges. There will be those who resist change. They will lose. One cannot stop the inevitable. God marches on. So too must we. There will always be more questions. There will always be more obstacles. Some things are never known. Questions drag us further. Theology guides us on. In the darkness, there is a still small futuristic voice calling us home. We will be alright if we dare to listen.

Is resistance futile?

"Push!" They didn't know if they could make it. "Squeeze!" Knowing that it was going to come out of them eventually, they all held to each other as tight as they could. Love seemed to be what was keeping them together. "One more push!" They kept clinging. "Keep pushing!" After a few more screams, beauty finally arrived. "Oh my!" The pain melted away. Looking deeply into the ball, they were amazed by the colors that exploded. With all the gathered listening intently, the Holy Trinity declared that the ball would be called, "Earth." They also announced their name on Earth, "God." Ever since then, the Holy Trinity has looked over the world. Since the beginning, countless creatures have filled the ball. As they looked down upon that which was made, the Holy Trinity declared, "There is nothing more fulfilling or painful than birthing a planet." In the span of eternity, God never stops birthing. The universe keeps going. The will be about meeting other planets. Our future will be about meeting other Gods who we will discover to be the same as ours.

Who birthed God?

Mutations occur throughout nature. Perhaps, pollution and other factors will bring about extreme mutations in us. What will we do with mutations that scare us? It is scary when someone is able to read you mind. It is scary when someone is born stronger than anyone else. It is scary when someone has an ability to see through things. We have no idea what the human body is capable of. Mutations will show us the way. Jesus was a mutant. Sinless living and miraculous powers are certainly a mutation in comparison with other humans. How can we blame the Pharisees for being afraid of a mutant when we would be too? Jesus shows us what a mutant can look like. Maybe she is not alone?

Is God a mutant?

"Bring that one over here." "Are you talking about the one in the second cabinet?" "Yes, son." "Bring it over here! It's ready to hatch." They put the egg in the incubator and stepped back. As the egg started to tremble, a crack developed. The crack grew bigger and bigger until a small explosion occured. A ball popped out. Holding it tightly, the father showed it to his son. When his wife walked in, the father showed it to her too. Nobody could believe it. The ball was already growing. After a second, they knew it was time. Father ran over and opened the roof. Space was so close. The ball grew bigger and bigger. Eventually, they let the ball go. The ball drifted up and out to space. The family wept. They wondered if they would ever see it again. Little did they know, the creatures would spend tremendous amounts of energy from their creation on seeking to know their God. In time, God learned how to talk back. I wonder if we will?

How would you like your eggs?

There was a force that bound them together. Deep inside, they always knew what to do. They knew they were to build a planet. Every day, they did something different. One of them put the animals in place. One of them put the oceans in place. One put the land in place. There were many tasks to do. They kept working until it was done. As they were about to finish, the force that bound them all together said, "Now, I want you to make humans in our image. Let's show each other what to do." In time, they constructed billions of humans. When the time came, they let them free. For just a moment, they surveyed the work they'd done and declared it good. With a long hop, they all jumped back in the ship. Before they could close the door, they screamed as loud as they could, "I promise you we will be in touch." Over time, it became apparent . . . they were the purple God. Then they came back. What happens when we discover that God isn't necessarily what we thought God would be? Would we worship an alien? I guess God is an alien on some level. In the future, we will learn more about our creation. Are we prepared for some of our assumptions to be wrong?

Do you ever create outside of our world?

When did these events happen? Time seems to become irrelevant when you are talking about beginnings. Was something created in the future and brought back to the past? What is the future and what is the past? Was something created in the past and brought to the future? Beginnings always seem to have a tremendous consequence on the present. It seems we bring them forward all the time or perhaps we go back. I'm not sure. I just know that beginnings stay with us. Beginnings are both the future and the past. Beginnings are timeless. Though we configure and construct them in a variety of ways, we are still searching for the beginning. Perhaps, every generation constructs beginnings differently. Could it be that such constructions are what carry us into the future? I think so.

Where does God begin?

Police violence is only getting worse. When you put a gun on someone's hip, they become superman. Does Jesus believe in police? Is a world without police even possible? Maybe. However, I don't think that's the direction we're headed. With the introduction of automated speed enforcement, it doesn't seem irrational to think that policing will become totally automated. How do you hold a robot accountable for police brutality? When robots can cast judgment in the streets, totalitarianism is always next. Someone will control the robots.

Will the police destroy us?

Factories are closing. Production processes are becoming more and more automated. Where is God when people are losing their jobs? How can people support themselves when there is no work? The future seems to be about the destruction of the workforce. What will we do? Perhaps, the only way to move forward is to create. In the future, we will find ourselves emulating God. We will be the creator in order to survive. Maybe that's how God survives. Creation is life and life is creation.

What is work?

God lives in creation. Creation lives in God. Concepts of God are based on the conception of the thinker. Doesn't every thinker think from their self? Such thoughts get explanatory when you start to consider how we think. God comes out of the source of the thought. The conclusion that we are made in God's image goes both ways. It explains who we are. It also explains who God is. If we are made in the image of God then God is made in the image of us. So, if you create life then the life you create is made in your image. When you have a child, you share countless characteristics. The child is made in your image. When you go even further and think about the many other movements of creation, you begin to realize just how these images experience exponential growth in every second. The image of God extends to spaces we've never dreamed of.

Is creation real?

No one had ever even thought to even try such a journey before. Blasting off into the unknown, the explorers raced through space. There was no hope they'd ever make it back. This was a suicide mission. The goal was to create knowledge and send back as much as they could. Darkness engulfed everything. They were tasked with engaging deep space and they did. After years of searching, the explorers arrived at the perfect planet. The new black ball was just hanging there. There was no life in it all. It was formless. One of the explorers had a special gift. Sometimes the other explorers called her God. They were amazed at her abilities. After putting her gear on, she walked out onto the wing and extended hear hands high above his head. With the snap of her right fingers, the heavens appeared. With a snap of her left fingers, the earth appeared. She stepped back to admire all that she'd done. The heavens and earth were here. The crew agreed to call it "Earth 2." After the mission was complete, the crew kept going. The explorer shared how to create. Before she knew it, everyone was creating heavens and earths. They realized that anyone can create. On each planet, numerous intelligent creatures were put in charge. The explorers found their existence in creation. When they were through, they laid down to die together. That's all they thought there was left to do. As they closed their eyes, memories of the 4,863 planets they'd created came rushing back. Along their journey, one doubt remained. Should they be creating so much? In time, the answer became clearer and clearer. The beginning never ends.

Does a new creation require a new God?

Would you live differently if you knew someone was watching you all the time? Is God watching us? Many people say so. Regardless, what if it wasn't God watching us? What if it was our governments or other non-government institutions? Invasions of privacy are becoming more and more frequent. When will enough be enough? Will we give so much away that there is no turning back? Maybe we already have? I have no doubt that in the future institutions will only try to go further. Will we choose to be like God and watch?

Who is watching God?

The materials just sat there. Frightened by what might happen, the scientist didn't dare put his ideas in action. However, the temptation remained. Everyday, the scientist would stop and ponder about what could be. One day, the scientist finally succumbed to the temptation. The formless materials would be formless no more. The scientist was very cautious. Darkness could slip in very easily. When the scientist was finished, the creation arose. The creation was identical to a human. The creation was the most advanced piece of artificial intelligence ever created. Then came the sound of a mighty wind. The creation started to twitch and fell to the floor. When the scientist reached the creation, he dove into the floor to make sure he was ok. In that moment, the scientist breathed life into the creation. The souls of creator and creation were one. The connection caused an enormous burst of light. Nothing bigger had ever happened.

Did God have to be assembled?

If you could be cured of a mental illness, would you want to be? Is there not perfection in defection? If one is created in God's image, would mental illness not be part of such creation? Who decides what needs to be cured? More cures are coming. Everyone will have to personally decide what needs to be cured. Ever consider that wearing glasses might one day be seen as an act of rebellion? What if we develop the means to fix everyone's vision? Glasses will become obsolete. Oppression will come for those who dare to be different? But what if you like wearing glasses? In the future, difference could be treasonous.

Is divinity crazy?

After decades of perfecting their light machine, dozens of scientists came together to see if it actually worked. After broadcasting the proper warning to peoples around the world, the scientists started the countdown. At first, the machine didn't start up. For a few hours, the scientists tinkered to see what was wrong. To the surprise of everyone in attendance and the countless people watching at home, the machine started. All of a sudden, the entire hemisphere darkened. Nobody could believe that it actually worked. The scientists slapped hands and jumped up and down. For the first time, scientists were able to divide light from the darkness and vice versa. Day and night were now firmly controlled. Who could have ever believed that it would be possible to control day and night?

Are we day or are we night?

Radiological blasts were pummeling the planet. People had never felt anything like it. Every few days, a new catastrophe exploded. People got sicker and sicker. Water was in short supply. Terrorism could no longer be contained. People around the planet begged their leaders to figure something out. The space station capable of holding humanity was not ready yet. Time was running out. The planet was terminal. Just when it all seemed over, a technology firm deployed a device they called firmament. As it wrapped the planet, the device created a protective shield to protect the planet from the harshness of space. Though it would only work for just a little while, it was enough time to save the planet. Humanity was saved from themselves. Before there was chaos and now there was peace. Stabilization ushered in heaven.

Is our time running out?

Are jails necessary? What if it was truly possible to completely reform someone? Maybe a reform machine will be developed? What if punishment was nothing more than being changed? If our future is to better than our past, we will find a way to destroy jails and create a society that believes in reform. There is no future if we keep locking each other up. If we continue to go the way of jails, we will eventually all be locked up. Real change is possible. God is always trying to break us out of our habits of destroying the lives of others. We must refrain from locking up the future.

Would God bust out of jail?

Eventually, people started to believe that oceans were holding humanity back. The population was exploding and there was nowhere else to go. Thinkers of all stripes came together and started to work on a solution. They had to figure out a way to turn water into land. Experiment after experiment went wrong. Numerous people gave their lives to advance the cause. One day a student brought a vile of chemicals that he thought might work. The other thinkers were dismissive until the student walked out in front of them and made land shoot out from the shore. It was a miracle. In time, everyone enjoyed plenty of land. Unfortunately, humanity became aggressive in their desire for land and depleted all of the water. Now, they were faced with a different set of problems. How would they bring water back? Creation has its downfalls.

Does water make us human?

What happens when water dies? Humanity cannot live. We must have water. Shortages of water will lead to wars over water. There is already scarcity throughout the world. The regions that are suffering the most are those that have the least. Water shortages kill the oppressed and marginalized first. How are we to be the purveyors of the waters of life when we don't have any water to give? Living water is water that keeps you alive. If we don't have it, where will our salvation come from?

Has God evaporated?

The seas rose higher and higher. Before everyone knew it, water was all that was left. Humanity was left to survive on docks and floats and boats. While you couldn't say they flourished, you could say that they never stopped surviving. A doctor in a floating medical laboratory began to wonder if it was possible to make the human body better suited for the water. After many drawings, thoughts and prototypes, the doctor believed he'd come up with something. A woman volunteered to be the doctor's first patient. Over the course of two days, the doctor fitted her with prosthetic gills in her neck, scales on her skin and webbing on her feet. After her recovery, the woman jumped off the laboratory and was able to swim and stay underwater for very long distances. When people started to hear what the doctor could do, everyone wanted the surgery. After other doctors were trained, humanity began to move underwater. Cities were constructed at the bottom of the ocean. Creation led to creation. The people called the water . . . home and everything above the surface . . . sky.

Are we willing to radically transform?

The leaders of the galaxy came together and decided to reimagine weapons of mass destruction. Together, they wanted to find a way to create weapons of mass construction. The top thinkers in the galaxy came together on an isolated moon and went to work. While the force of the weapons could remain, the contents of the weapons had to change. The thinkers went round and round. Cultures clashed and compromises were ultimately reached. When the weapons were complete, the thinkers called them weapons of life. After affixing them to thruster systems, the thinkers partnered with the leaders of the galaxy to shoot these weapons toward planet after planet. Upon impact, grass began to grow, vegetables took form, herbs filled the fields, fruit trees multiplied and all sorts of creatures suited for the environment started to swarm. Unexpectedly, new species of intelligent life developed. The thinkers and the leaders were now creators of creation. The decision was made to back off and let them develop on their own. In six different spaces, the same thing happened . . . life. They all were amazed at how quickly the very different intelligent species grew and changed. Evolution was stark. Who could have imagined that weapons would bring about the future?

Are there answers in the stars?

Strange lights appeared in the sky. All over the world, people couldn't figure out what was going on. Governments wondered whether to come forward and tell everyone. Then, a scientist came out in a worldwide telecast and apologized for causing alarm. The scientist revealed that for decades he had led a team of scientists that were charged with creating artificial stars. A few weeks ago, their efforts had paid off and they began creating new stars. Everyone was happy that it wasn't something else. The stars became a home for messages and wonder. There was always light when it was needed. Quickly, the light became very helpful in engaging catastrophes and all sorts of events of mass need. Though everything was good for a little while, it didn't take long until countries started fighting over the technology. Stars filled up the sky and provide too much light. People started to get burned in different parts of the world. Everyone knew that there was a problem, but nobody would come together to fix it. The creation quickly became a problem. Light grew more evil by the day.

Is darkness light?

Children are often put in circumstances that make them grow up fast. We look at such situations as a problem. We assume that such children are unhealthy. What if we're wrong? What if technology was produced that could make children grew up at faster rates? Would you want you child to experience it? Advanced education could being much earlier. Work could begin much earlier. Families could begin much earlier. Everything would begin much earlier. Could this be a part of our future? Maybe it already is.

Is God a child?

Ready for a new look, Ray decided he was going to get some cosmetic surgery. After looking through every piece of literature he could find, Ray went to a renowned local cosmetic surgeon and asked about a private appointment. Though he didn't have any money, the doctor took him on. Ray decided he wanted two specific alterations. A few weeks later, Ray pulled up. Extremely nervous, Ray walked through the door and sat down. After an exchange of pleasantries, Ray started outlining what he wanted. "I would like a really big functional eye in my forehead. I will call it the greater light. I would also like a small functional eye in the back of my head. I will call it the lesser light." The doctor thought for a second and shared that the technology exists to make it happen. After a couple of inquiries and warnings, the doctor gave Ray a date for surgery. When the day arrived, Ray was suspended above the floor and temporarily paralyzed. The anesthesia was just a precaution/backup. When Ray awoke, he was unable to see the results for a few days. When the medical team finally removed the bandages, Ray was overwhelmed. He could see in every direction. Throwing his fists in the air, Ray screamed, "I once was blind but now I see!"

Has God had cosmetic enhancements?

Darkness engulfed everything. No one could find the source. Unable to find an easy solution, scientists went to work. Using technology that had been previously developed, they created a mechanism that would give everyone left on the planet night vision. The spray was dropped all over the world. People shot the spray right into their eyes. Apart from the minor bleeding, everyone was happy to see again. Together, people all over the world were able to divide light from darkness. Although the colors were different, people were just happy they could see.

Can God see?

How will you know the future? Spiritual sight is a prerequisite. If you cannot see, your hope is gone. There is no future without hope. Our lives are about grabbing hope and riding it into the future for as long as we can. If we fall off, I bet that God is capable of opening our eyes. God is hope. God is our future.

Is sight possible?

Pollution had finally done the planet in. The oceans were so dirty that waves of dead fish constantly landed on shore. Lakes were so toxic that boats would slowly disintegrate in the water. Rain was the worst of all. Every drop felt like fire. Burns were so common that people couldn't go to a hospital for them and they were told to deal with them at home. Though scientists around the world were working on a solution, an isolated and forgotten biomedical engineer came up with a solution . . . after many tests . . . it failed. Humanity perished.

Is God choking?

Extreme breeding programs were developed to create perfect animals. From horses to dogs to insects to whales, all types of animals were tested to find the perfect characteristics. Unfortunately, the programs got out of control and many animals became endangered. Frightened about what could happen, a doctoral student used various hypotheses and processes she'd been working on to create perfect animals in a lab. The process involved genes and light swirling around in a colossal tube. Instantly, the type of animal you desire pops out. On some level, it works just like a microwave. Birds had not been seen in years. Now there were millions and millions and millions of them of every size and color . . . filling every corner of the earth. Everyone rejoiced at the new development. The songs and shrieks that filled the air were divine. After experimenting with every animal on the planet, the breeding programs turned to recreating extinct animals. Within a few years, breeders created dinosaurs, woolly mammoths and all sorts of exotic extinct creatures. The earth began to fill with creatures. Large formerly extinct whales and fish filled the oceans. Engagement with all of these different species made breeders turn to mythical species. Unicorns and Loch-Ness Monsters started to roam the planet as well. Since all of these animals drank and ate everything they could find, sustenance became an issue. Many communities didn't know what to do. Some wondered why God would give them the ability to create in the first place.

Can God be bred?

Why does God give us the ability to destroy ourselves? Does God not care about our future? Is God actively working against us? Does God enjoy seeing us fail? Perhaps, God created the future to watch us suffer? While I don't want to believe it, maybe that's the only explanation?

Are we being hunted?

After many years of development, a new incredibly advanced generation of robots was born. Identical to humans in every way, most communities were amazed that they truly had no idea who was artificial and who was not. Capable of reproduction, the robots became fruitful and multiplied. In addition to procreating with each other, robots started to procreate with humans. A new race of beings were born . . . half artificial and half human. Slowly, robots grew smarter and smarter. As their numbers grew past the numbers of humans, robots started to discriminate against humans. Violence followed. In need of somewhere to escape to, humans started to fill the waters of the seas and the heavens of the air. Nowhere felt safe. It wasn't long before everyone realized that they needed to leave. After a huge airlift of the remaining humans, they settled on the first inhabitable planet they could find. Cognizant of their prior troubles, humans decided to not create any robots again.

Will we kill the robots?

What is beyond a penis and a vagina? We already know that people are born intersex or with a sexual organ that is altogether different. What if something beyond our present ideas of sexual organs was created? What if it became possible to pleasure someone or procreate in a variety of different ways? Would God be in the midst of such creation? Are we only relegated to variations of the dichotomy that we already know? Will sex toys become so advanced that they become a part of our physical constitution? God promotes love. How could God not promote enhanced lovemaking? God is in our sex and sex is in our God. May the future be pleasurable!

Is there a divine sexual organ?

Globalization is everywhere. We are learning more and more about a variety of other peoples. Will such interactions destroy cultures our enhance them? We have already seen what happens when appropriation is unleashed. The constitution of people will die. How do we protect the things we most hold dear when everybody is stealing everything? Why doesn't God protect the queerness of creation? Does God care? I thought God was in all cultures? When we appropriate other cultures aren't destroying God? Is globalization killing God? Culture is a holy thing.

What happens when God kills cultures?

Is it possible to erase evil? What if we get to a point where we can erase what we have done and start over? Why doesn't God do this? The scriptures talk about sin often. If we are able to erase our own sin, doesn't that make scripture's discussion of evil obsolete? Think about being your own confessor and redeemer. Why would you need Jesus? It will be interesting to see how we respond when our sacraments become technologized. I guess this has happened throughout the history of the church. Isn't it happening right now? The churches that survive will see the future as the fruit of God not the death God.

Is God evil?

You open the door. Darkness is all that you see. You take one step and begin to fall. Fear is all that you know. Then, you see a light.

It is as if the light is guiding you forward. You realize that you are not alone. God is guiding you to the light. The further you fall the closer you get to the future. While God should be questioned about the future, we must never forget that God is falling too. The future is a fall and the fall is God.

> *How does God know?*
> *Where will God go?*
> *God is the question.*
> *God is the future.*

Postscript

How will it end? Surely, the future has an end. Perhaps, we're racing to nothing. If so, God is nothing. For, we cannot resist the pull of creation. We are from nothing and to nothing we shall return. In our race to nothing, we discover that nothing is eternal. The absence of things is everything. For those who fear tomorrow, I encourage you to let go . . . the future is nothing.

POSTSCRIPT

www.ingramcontent.com/pod-product-compliance
Lightning Source LLC
Chambersburg PA
CBHW070749050426
42449CB00010B/2397